The Quiet Unfolding

Poems of Surrender and Awakening

Elizabeth Caron

BookLeaf Publishing

India | USA | UK

Made with ❤ on the BookLeaf Publishing Platform

www.bookleafpub.in

www.bookleafpub.com

Dedication

To the people I have loved,
 whose hearts intertwined with mine,
 you taught me the art of connection,
 the joy of giving, the sorrow of parting.

Our paths have crossed and diverged,
 but each step with you
 has shaped who I am,
 and who I am becoming.

To those who have loved me,
 with patience, kindness, and unwavering belief,
 you have been my anchors in the storm,
 my light in the darkness.
 In your love, I learned to see myself,
 not as I was, but as I could be.

To the beauty of self-discovery,
 the quiet unfolding of who we are
 beneath the layers we once wore,
 thank you for the courage to shed the past,
 for the strength to walk alone
 and yet never truly be alone.

To letting go,
for teaching me that release is not loss,
but the freedom to rise again,
to make space for new growth,
new love, and new truths.

May we always remember
that the most profound love
begins within.

Preface

The Quiet Unfolding is a collection born from the delicate dance between love and loss, growth and surrender. It is a reflection of the journey each of us takes toward self-awareness and transformation—often silent, often slow, but always unfolding.

These poems were written for those who have touched my life in profound ways—the ones I have loved, the ones who have loved me, and even those whose paths diverged from mine. Each person has been a mirror, reflecting parts of myself I had yet to discover, and through them, I've learned the intricate balance between holding on and letting go.

In this collection, you will find echoes of the beauty found in stillness, the quiet moments where life moves beneath the surface, shaping and shifting without our awareness. There is also a reckoning with the pain that comes from surrendering what no longer serves us— whether it's a relationship, an old identity, or the fear that holds us back from becoming who we truly are.

The Quiet Unfolding is not just about personal reflection, but about the larger journey we all share. It is about embracing the rhythm of the universe, understanding that growth comes in waves, and that healing is a process of gentle transformation. The poems here are an invitation to witness that process—not just as a reader, but as a fellow traveler on this path of discovery.

May these words serve as a reminder that every ending holds the seed of a new beginning. And in the quiet spaces between, we find the courage to bloom.

Acknowledgements

To Jackson, your support and belief in me have been a constant light.

To Jacob, thank you for your patience and understanding.

And to my mother, Barbara, your love and wisdom have shaped me in ways I can never fully repay.

This book is a reflection of the strength and inspiration you all provide me every day.

1. A New Dawn

The past is a shadow, heavy and long,
A place where I lingered, though I didn't belong.
Your words once a comfort, your touch once a balm,
Now they echo with chaos, no peace, no calm.

I've walked through the storm, felt its cruel rain,
The weight of the wounds, the shackles of pain.
But here, in this moment, I choose to be free,
To rise from the ashes and reclaim the real me.

No longer a victim, no longer defined,
By a love that was broken, by a heart that was blind.
The future ahead is mine to create,
A path of my choosing, a chance to reshape.

I will heal the bruises, the scars on my soul,
Embrace my own power, regain full control.
For though the night's dark and the journey's not clear,
Hope is the light that will guide me from here.

I'll stand tall in the morning, with strength in my chest,
No longer bound by what's left of the rest.
A new dawn is waiting, and I'll walk toward the sun,
For I've found the courage to finally be done.

2. The Steady Path

Integrity stands like a mountain tall,
  Unmoved by whispers, unmoved by the fall.
  Its roots are deep, its core is strong,
  A quiet hymn, a steadfast song.

Faith walks with it, hand in hand,
  Guiding the heart through shifting sand.
  Not fleeting hope, but steady grace,
  A lantern bright in the darkest place.

Hard work lays each stone with care,
  A bridge to dreams that wait out there.
  With every effort, sweat, and strain,
  The seeds of promise drink the rain.

Patience whispers, "Not yet, but soon,"
  As time bends softly, like tides to the moon.
  Each moment a step, each step a climb,
  Where effort meets the hand of time.

And when the summit comes in view,
  The prize is sweeter, the sky more blue.
  For the path was honest, the journey long,
  And each step a verse in your victory song.

Hold fast to truth, to faith, to toil,
Through tempest winds and barren soil.
For what is earned through heart and grit
Shines eternal—it will not quit.

3. The Long Road

The road is quiet, the sky stretched wide,
No hand to hold, no place to hide.
Just the whispering wind, the crunch of stone,
A journey made in the depths of alone.

The way ahead is shrouded, unclear,
Each step a dance with doubt and fear.
But somewhere deep, a spark remains,
A voice that whispers through the pain.

"You've walked this far; don't turn around,
There's light ahead, though it's not yet found.
Each step you take, though slow, unsure,
Is carving a path, is finding the cure."

The stars become your guiding friend,
Their silent watch a love they lend.
The moonlight bathes the weary trail,
A quiet promise—you will prevail.

Though shadows stretch and echoes call,
Though the weight of loneliness starts to fall,
Your heart keeps beating, your fire stays bright,
A beacon cutting through endless night.

And as the road winds toward the sun,
You'll see the journey has just begun.
For every mile, each tear, each strain,
Grew strength in you, forged through the pain.

The way is long, but it's yours to take,
With every step, a world you make.
So walk on, wanderer, find your place—
The road may be lonely, but it leads to grace.

4. The Quiet Rise

From the ashes, I rise, a glow in the dust,
Not with thunder, but with quiet trust.
The flames once raged, they burned me through,
But from their heat, I was born anew.

No fanfare needed, no grand display,
Just steady wings to greet the day.
Each feather forged in trials past,
Each breath a triumph, built to last.

The world may not stop, may not take note,
Of the fire I tamed, the battles I wrote.
But in my chest, a calm refrain,
A song of strength born from the pain.

I see the scars, and I do not weep—
They're proof of depths I dared to keep.
They mark the places I would not fall,
Where I stood again, and stood tall.

So I applaud in the silence, a soft ovation,
For my own quiet transformation.
No need for praise, no need for cheers—
I know the worth of these fought-for years.

Like the phoenix, I rise, my own light to see,
Not for the world, but for me—for me.
A quiet triumph, a whispered flame,
I stand anew, unbound, untamed.

5. Rise Again, My Soul

Rise again, my soul,
From the ashes of doubt,
Let the winds of courage lift you high,
And banish the shadows out.

Learn to fly, unbroken,
Like the eagle in the sky,
With wings of strength and freedom,
Daring to soar, to fly.

No longer bound by fear,
No longer held by the past,
Let your spirit glide on the breeze,
For you were born to outlast.

Dare to soar above the storms,
Let your heart be the guide,
In the vast expanse of the unknown,
Let your spirit take the ride.

With each beat of your wings,
Let the world see your fire,
For you are meant to conquer,
To rise, to dream, to inspire.

So rise again, my soul,
　Embrace the boundless sky,
　Learn to fly, and dare to soar—
　For you were meant to fly.

6. I Forgive You, My Love

In the quiet of the stars,
 I whisper to the moon,
 I forgive you, my love,
 For the silence and the gloom.

For the moments lost in shadows,
 For the words that never bloomed,
 I forgive you for the distance,
 For the heartache we've consumed.

I forgive you in the stillness,
 Where time itself slips away,
 In the breath between the night and dawn,
 I find peace, and here I stay.

I forgive you for the storms,
 For the nights we walked alone,
 For the spaces in our silence,
 Where love's light had not yet shone.

I forgive you in the whisper
 Of the wind's soft, fleeting touch,
 In the depth of the ocean's sigh,
 Where the soul remembers much.

I forgive you as the twilight falls,
  With stars in endless dance,
  For in this quiet moment, love,
  I give us one more chance.

I forgive you like the rain,
  That kisses earth with gentle grace,
  Washing away the wounds we bore,
  And leaving no trace.

So here, my love, I release you,
  To the heavens, to the sea,
  In the softness of the ether,
  I forgive you, and I am free.

7. In Your Eyes

In your eyes, I see
  The vastness of the ocean,
  Waves crashing against the rocks,
  Forever reshaping,
  Endlessly changing.

I see jungles wrapped in fog,
  Hiding secrets of ancient civilizations,
  Silent and untouched,
  Shielded from the chaos of the world.

I see mountains,
  Their peaks forever crowned in snow,
  Begging the sun to touch them,
  To grant them warmth,
  To offer them hope.

I see a lake,
  Frozen under the weight of the gales,
  Yet melting in the presence of our love,
  Thawing beneath our touch.

In those eyes, I see barefoot children,
  Journeying to a shack they call school,

Thirsting for knowledge,
For words to guide them.

I see zebras,
Dancing their survival dance,
Hiding from the lions' gaze,
Fighting to stay free.

I see waterfalls—
Gentle and forceful,
Kissing the ground,
Leaving their mark upon the earth.

Your eyes show me the world,
They make me live a thousand lives.
They reveal the secrets of your soul,
The only place where I long to hide,
Unbothered by the world's noise,

Listening only to the rhythm of your heartbeat.

8. The Quiet Echo

In the silence where love once sang,
 a tender ache softly clings.
 The air hums with what might have been,
 a melody of fractured strings.

Healing comes not swift, nor clean—
 it creeps like dawn through heavy mist.
 Each scar a map of dreams undone,
 each tear a wish we still resist.

I sit with the ghosts of what was us,
 their whispers kind, yet sharp and clear.
 They tell of love that still remains,
 though your absence cuts too near.

It wasn't enough—our reaching hands,
 the promises traced in trembling air.
 You hurt me, yes, but I can't unlove,
 the person I knew, the heart I shared.

Regret blooms in the quiet corners,
 where truth and hope no longer meet.
 I wanted more, I wanted forever—
 but some fires yield to retreat.

Still, I wish the stars to light your way,
  to guide your steps where mine cannot.
  Though we broke, I want your joy—
  a gift I carry, though time forgot.

This pain, a testament to love's pure weight,
  a wound that healing never hides.
  For even as I learn to let go,
  you remain a shadow in my tides.

9. Ownership of Self

You don't fear failure, not truly,
　You fear the whispers, the judgment, the view.
　The weight of others' eyes, their voices so loud,
　Their expectations, a shroud.

But ask yourself, what is failure to you?
　Is it falling short of a dream you never knew?
　Or is it the echoes of someone else's mind,
　A voice that's not yours, one you can't leave behind?

Failure, to me, is not the fall,
　It's not the stumble, the misstep, the call.
　It's the moment you stop, the choice not to learn,
　The fear that binds, the bridge you don't burn.

If my business falters, or love turns cold,
　I ask, what choices led me here, uncontrolled?
　What steps did I take, with eyes closed tight?
　What patterns repeat in the fading light?

For every frustration, every wrong,
　There's a lesson waiting, a place to belong.
　What can I learn, what truth can I see,
　To shift my course, to set myself free?

Ownership, my friend, is the key,
  To face the mirror and truly see.
  The power within, the strength to rise,
  To change my path, to claim the skies.

Each choice, each step, each word I own,
  Shaping my future, as seeds are sown.
  In every setback, in every doubt,
  I find the chance to turn it about.

So fear not failure, for it's just a guide,
  A moment to learn, to shift and collide.
  For in ownership, there's endless grace,
  And in each failure, I find my place.

10. Roots of Being

An awakened soul moves with grace,
Spontaneous, untouched by time or place.
Not bound by the chains of pretense or guise,
But flowing with truth in all that lies inside.

There's no need to force, to strive, to mold,
For the deepest truths cannot be told.
They live within, in silence and bloom,
A garden growing in the quietest room.

The roots are where it all begins,
Deep within, where life spins.
Watered with presence, nourished by love,
They reach for the sky, they rise above.

The branches stretch without demand,
Fingers to the heavens, rooted in the land.
The leaves unfold as the seasons change,
In effortless beauty, they rearrange.

Cultivate the roots, and trust in the flow,
The leaves will follow, the branches will grow.
No need to hurry, no need to pretend,
Just be, and the journey will never end.

The tree of life is simple and free,
In its own rhythm, it learns to be.
For when you are rooted in your truth,
The world around you will know your youth.

11. Blooming After Rain

An awakened soul moves with grace,
Spontaneous, untouched by time or place.
Not bound by the chains of pretense or guise,
But flowing with truth in all that lies inside.
There's no need to force, to strive, to mold,
For the deepest truths cannot be told.
They live within, in silence and bloom,
A garden growing in the quietest room.

The roots are where it all begins,
Deep within, where life spins.
Watered with presence, nourished by love,
They reach for the sky, they rise above.

The branches stretch without demand,
Fingers to the heavens, rooted in the land.
The leaves unfold as the seasons change,
In effortless beauty, they rearrange.

Cultivate the roots, and trust in the flow,
The leaves will follow, the branches will grow.

No need to hurry, no need to pretend,
Just be, and the journey will never end.

The tree of life is simple and free,
In its own rhythm, it learns to be.
For when you are rooted in your truth,
The world around you will know your youth.

12. Where Love Grows

It began as a whisper, a seedling thought,
 a flicker of warmth where shadows fought.
 Your presence, gentle, soft, and near,
 like sunlight breaking through doubt and fear.

At first, the petals stayed curled tight,
 unsure of the day, wary of the night.
 But your voice, like rain, so steady and kind,
 nurtured the soil of my hesitant mind.

Each glance, each touch, a tender glow,
 coaxing the flower to stretch, to grow.
 With every word, with every smile,
 I opened further, mile by mile.

The stem grew strong, the leaves took form,
 a love so quiet, yet lush and warm.
 One petal unfurled, then another still,
 a testament to your patient will.

Now, fully open, this love has grown,
 a bloom we've nurtured, a life we've sown.
 Its colors vivid, its fragrance true,
 a garden thriving with me and you.

No storm can steal this blossom's grace,
no wind can tear its rooted place.
For in your arms, I've come to see—
this love, this flower, was meant to be.

13. Rebirth of the Flame

From the ashes, I rise,
A phoenix reborn with open skies.
The flames that once consumed my soul,
Now fuel the fire that makes me whole.

I spread my wings, so wide, so free,
Leaving behind the wreckage of what used to be.
The smoke that once clouded my sight,
Now clears, and I embrace the light.

Each feather forged in fire's embrace,
I carry strength, I carry grace.
The scars upon my body tell
A story of a life that fell,
But in the fall, I learned to fly,
A spirit unbroken, reaching high.

With every breath, I rise again,
A force of nature, free from sin.
The darkness may try to pull me low,
But from the ashes, I will grow.

A new dawn breaks, the sun will shine,
And I will walk this path divine.

The phoenix soars, through skies so bright,
A symbol of resilience, of endless fight.

25

No longer bound by what was lost,
I rise above, no matter the cost.
For in my heart, the fire burns,
A light that guides, a soul that learns.

14. Let Them

Let them doubt, let them sneer,
 Let them question why you're here.
 Let their whispers fill the air—
 Your strength was born of what they dare.

Let them watch as you unfold,
 Turning wounds to veins of gold.
 Let them wonder, let them wait—
 You shape the locks, you hold the gate.

Let them mock the dreams you chase,
 Call you reckless, out of place.
 Let them miss the truth you know—
 The seeds of courage always grow.

Let them leave, let them stay,
 Let them find their own lost way.
 Their paths are theirs, their burdens too,
 Yours is a journey they can't construe.

Let them see your rising flame,
 A soul unbound, a heart untamed.
 Let them marvel, let them yearn,
 Let them grow, or let them learn.

Let them go, if they must,
  Love, like tides, will test our trust.
  But let them never take from you—
  The light that's fierce, the love that's true.

But let them never steal your grace—
  A soul unyielding, time won't erase.

15. Let Me

Let me own my truth, stand tall,
No more shrinking, no more small.
Let me rise where I belong,
Unapologetic, fierce, and strong.

Let me break the chains I've known,
Carve new paths, walk alone.
Let me chase what sets me free,
A life that's truly meant for me.

Let me learn, let me fail,
Let me weather every gale.
Every stumble, every scar,
Guides me closer to my star.

Let me blossom, let me grow,
In my time, at my own flow.
Not a petal forced to bend,
But a garden with no end.

Let me love—first myself,
Not as a whisper, but in full health.
A fire burning, bright and true,
So love may shine in all I do.

Let me dream beyond the sky,
Unbound by fear, let me fly.
Let me, always, dare to be—
The fullest, truest version of me.

16. Like Water

Water flows without a sound,
Embracing each curve, every bound.
It moves with ease, with gentle grace,
Finding its way, no need to chase.

In stillness, it reflects the sky,
In motion, it whispers as it passes by.
Neither rushing nor slowing its pace,
It simply follows its destined place.

It moves through life with quiet might,
Guiding without force, in soft delight.
It's in the river's endless song,
In the mountain, where it has belonged.

In every drop that kisses earth,
In every seed, in every birth,
Water shapes the world with care,
Without a plan, without a prayer.

It carves the stones, smooths the rough,
Teaching us that we are enough.
So let go, let your soul decide,
Like water, let your heart glide.

Move with grace, with no resistance,
And find the peace in true existence.

17. Whispers of the Forest

In the heart of the forest, where whispers are deep,
The trees stand as guardians, quiet and steep.
The leaves softly murmur, a lullaby's song,
As the world fades away, and the moments belong.

The air is a blanket, gentle and kind,
It wraps 'round your soul, leaving worries behind.
Each step on the earth is a rhythm, a dance,
A breath in the silence, a calm, steady trance.

The brook sings its stories, the birds gently call,
In this sacred stillness, you're part of it all.
The rustle of branches, the crackle of pine,
All rhythms of nature, in perfect design.

Here in the forest, all anxious thoughts cease,
The heart finds its rhythm, the mind finds its peace.
A world full of wonder, where time stands so still,
In the embrace of the forest, my spirit can heal.

18. Spring to My Soul

The stream bubbles softly, a song in its flow,
 Carrying secrets where wildflowers grow.
 It dances on pebbles, so light and so free,
 A melody woven in nature's decree.

The flowers beside it, with colors so bright,
 Unfurl like the dawn, breaking through night.
 Their petals like whispers, their fragrance so pure,
 They awaken my spirit, of that I am sure.

Each bloom is a promise, each breath is a prayer,
 The stream hums its joy in the warm spring air.
 With every petal, my heart feels reborn,
 Like spring to my soul, with each soft new morn.

The world in its stillness, the stream in its song,
 In nature's embrace, I feel I belong.
 For flowers are spring, and the stream is my guide,
 Together they carry my spirit inside.

19. The Canvas of My Soul

Art is the language my heart learns to speak,
 A brushstroke of silence, a whisper so sleek.
 It speaks of my struggles, my dreams, and my fears,
 Of moments in shadows, and shedding of tears.

Each color, a pulse; each shape, a release,
 A window, a doorway, where I find my peace.
 With every creation, I heal and I grow,
 The more I let go, the more I will know.

Through every canvas, my soul takes its flight,
 A journey of healing, of finding my light.
 The brush is my voice, the colors my song,
 In the realm of creation, I finally belong.

As my creativity blossoms, I rise from the dark,
 Art is the fire that ignites the spark.
 A reflection of me, yet ever anew,
 A tapestry woven, where life is made true.

20. Whispers of the Pine

The forest hums softly, a pulse I can feel,
  As I sit in the quiet, the world seems surreal.
  The pine needles cradle me, gentle and true,
  A blanket of comfort beneath skies so blue.

The breeze stirs the branches, a symphony's tune,
  While birds weave their stories beneath the bright
moon.
  Each rustle, a whisper, each sigh, a deep breath,
  The forest is alive, speaking of life and death.

I listen to secrets the earth softly keeps,
  As the energy of nature into my soul seeps.
  The trees sway in rhythm, the ground holds me tight,
  In this moment, all is peaceful, all is right.

Here, in the stillness, my spirit finds grace,
  The forest's true energy, a sacred space.
  With each breath I take, I become part of the sound,
  In the heart of the forest, I am truly found.

21. Gifts of the Forest

In the heart of the forest, where treasures unfold,
 Are gifts from the earth, both sacred and bold.
 Beneath the tall trees, through leaves soft and green,
 Nature's rich bounty, in each moment, is seen.

The pinecones, the stones, the bark's textured grace,
 Each element whispers, a truth to embrace.
 With every branch, every petal that falls,
 A lesson in patience, in answering calls.

From the earth comes abundance, from the sky comes
the light,
 A collection of blessings, both humble and bright.
 These gifts of the forest, a symbol so clear,
 Of healing and growth, of all we hold dear.

They lead to prosperity, not measured in gold,
 But in wisdom and peace, and stories untold.
 In each natural treasure, a journey begins,
 To a life full of balance, where healing begins.

As I gather these gifts, I too shall grow,
 My craft, my spirit, a thriving flow.
 For the forest has shown me, through each treasure

found,

The path to success is where peace is unbound.

www.ingramcontent.com/pod-product-compliance
Lightning Source LLC
La Vergne TN
LVHW021313200726
843509LV00012B/1899